Mollie Keller

ALEXANDER HAMILTON

Richard B. Morris, Consulting Editor

Franklin Watts   *1986*   *A First Book*
New York   *London*   *Toronto*   *Sydney*

For the memory of
my father,
who first introduced me to
Mr. Hamilton

All photographs courtesy of
The Bettmann Archive

Library of Congress Cataloging in Publication Data

Keller, Mollie.
Alexander Hamilton.

(A First book)
Bibliography: p.
Includes index.
Summary: A biography of the man who among other
achievements was a Revolutionary War hero, an aide and
advisor to George Washington, a framer of the
Constitution, and the first Secretary of the Treasury
of the newly formed United States.
1. Hamilton, Alexander, 1757–1804—Juvenile litera-
ture. 2. Statesmen—United States—Biography—Juvenile
literature. 3. United States—Politics and government
—1783–1809—Juvenile literature. [1. Hamilton,
Alexander, 1757–1804. 2. Statesmen]   I. Morris,
Richard Brandon, 1904–   . II. Title.
E302.6.H2K45 1986 973.4′092′4 [B] [92] 86-5670
ISBN 0-531-10214-9

Contents

Alexander Hamilton

Prologue

He stood about 5 feet 10 inches (178 cm) tall, although he had his coats cut long to make himself appear taller. His eyes were a dark blue-gray. He combed his reddish-brown hair back off his face, powdered it, and tied it in a low pony tail at his neck. Women found him charming, and uncommonly handsome. Men were impressed by his intelligence and seriousness.

He had come to New York as a poor youth to get a college education, but quickly made himself one of the most powerful and important men in America. He was a Revolutionary War hero, an aide and advisor to George Washington, a framer of the Constitution, and the nation's first secretary of the Treasury.

His name was Alexander Hamilton, and this is his story.

*Alexander Hamilton, Major General of the Armed Forces
of the United States of America, Secretary of the Treasury*

Chapter

1

The Islands

All children dream about what they are going to be when they grow up. Nowadays they plan on careers as astronauts, athletes, or rock stars. With hard work, good training, and a little bit of luck, many boys and girls today figure they have a good chance of living their dreams.

Children living a long time ago thought about their futures, too. In 1769 a twelve-year-old boy sat at a table in a small office on the West Indian island of St. Croix and poured his heart out in a letter to his best friend. He hated his job as a clerk in a general store, and he dreaded spending the rest of his life there. He wanted something more. "My Ambition is prevalent," he confessed. "I would willingly risk my life tho' not my Character to exalt my Station." Embarrassed about admitting his dreams of glory (he called it "building castles in the air"), the boy concluded his letter with one quick note: "I wish there was a War."

The boy who wrote this was Alexander Hamilton. His wish for war was a very practical one. To his thinking only some brilliant and heroic act on the battlefield would give him even a chance to achieve his hopes.

As drastic as his reasoning may seem today, it was pretty accurate. He did seem to be doomed to a life of clerking. For one thing, he was at the bottom of the social ladder. His parents, who had never married, separated when Hamilton was nine, and his mother was forced to support her two sons by running a grocery from one of the rooms in their tiny home. When she died two years later, the boys were all alone. There was not even a cousin who could afford to take them in.

Hamilton's future was also limited by his lack of schooling. Although he had learned to read and write both English and French while still quite young, and had picked up the basics of arithmetic from helping out in his mother's shop, his family had never lived anyplace long enough for him to go to a proper school. In fact, the only real school he ever attended was a Jewish one. There he learned to recite parts of the Bible in Hebrew, standing on the table to do so because he was so short.

The third obstacle that Fate had put in Hamilton's path was his location. Then, as now, the West Indies were a tropical paradise of lush green islands floating in turquoise blue waters. They owed their population and their prosperity to profits from the sugar and slave trades. But despite overflowing warehouses, bustling markets, and ports crowded with sailing ships, the islands were political and cultural backwaters, far removed from the European nations which governed them. To make matters worse for Hamilton, St. Croix was a Danish island. There was little chance there for a boy of Scotch and English parentage to ever achieve any important office.

So Alexander Hamilton faced his future with three strikes against him: no family, no education, and no room to grow. Yet he was determined to rise to the top. Fortunately he had one great gift that could overcome all his handicaps—genius. Left alone in the world, he turned his experience stocking the shelves of his mother's store to good use. He apprenticed himself to a well-to-do merchant named Nicholas Cruger and earned his room and board as he learned the grocery business.

He learned a lot more besides. He learned how to bargain, how to figure foreign exchange rates, and how to evade the hundreds of customs regulations that tied every cargo up in yards of red tape. Even though still in his teens, he was soon Cruger's second-in-command, and ran the business whenever his employer was away.

He also put his spare time to good use. When not at his desk figuring how to price forty barrels of spoiled flour so they would sell, he wrote sentimental love poems and fiery political essays. Many of these he saw published in the island newspaper.

It was his writing, in fact, that brought him his longed-for escape from the West Indies.

On the last night of August 1772, a violent hurricane tore across St. Croix. For three hours tremendous winds flattened houses, uprooted crops, and scattered livestock. As the eye of the storm passed over the island, people cautiously poked their heads out of doors and windows to view the damage, but soon the winds were back, howling and blowing harder than before. By morning thirty people had died. Ships lay broken on the shore like toy boats in an empty bathtub. The island was devastated.

Hamilton had stayed awake all night to watch the storm. The next day he tried to capture its fury with pen and ink. Even though he probably never intended to send it to anyone but the editor of the *Royal Danish-American Gazette*, he wrote his description as a letter to his father. The piece was very vivid and exciting. Hamilton wrote of "fiery meteors flying about in the air," of the "glare of almost perpetual lightning," and of the "ear-piercing shrieks of the distressed." To the fifteen-year-old boy, the storm was clearly a sign of God's wrath.

Hamilton's letter impressed his minister so much that he showed it to all his friends. He said it proved the boy's promise and he convinced them to contribute to his education.

Within a month of the hurricane Alexander Hamilton stood on the deck of a ship bound for North America. In the hold was a cargo of island products he had been given to sell. The profits were to pay for a "gentleman's education" at one of the colleges there. A self-reliant, self-taught, and self-assured youth, Hamilton watched with sorrow and excitement as the pink and white houses of St. Croix faded away. Perhaps now he would no longer have to content himself with building castles in the air. Maybe in America he could build a real one.

Chapter

2

College Boy

Hamilton's island education was not enough to earn him a place at an American college. He needed at least a year of study before he knew enough Latin, Greek, and mathematics to enter Harvard, Yale, or the College of New Jersey at Princeton.

Getting that extra schooling proved no problem for him. He had arrived in New York with letters of introduction to prominent citizens from Cruger and his minister. These people in turn introduced Hamilton to their friends and associates. One of these new acquaintances enrolled Hamilton in Dr. Barber's Academy in Elizabethtown, New Jersey.

Hamilton was very lucky to have the sponsors he did. They were the intellectual and social leaders of colonial life. After a childhood of poverty, at last he was living in one of his castles in the air.

Hamilton worked hard at his studies. He often stayed up past midnight doing his homework by candlelight. As spring turned into summer, he found he could add hours to his study time by waking early and taking his books with him to the nearby churchyard. There he would sit, leaning his back against some convenient tombstone, and prepare his lessons for the day ahead.

In 1773, after less than a year of study, he was ready for college. He decided to apply to Princeton, where so many of his new friends had gone, but that school would not let him devise his own curriculum. So Hamilton packed his books and clothes and ferried back across the Hudson to King's College (now Columbia University) in New York City, where he could proceed at his own speed.

Here he studied Latin and anatomy and hired a private tutor to guide him through business mathematics. Hamilton intended to become a doctor and worked even harder than he had at Dr. Barber's school. Long into the night he would pace back and forth across his room, muttering to himself as he solved some math problem or memorized the bones of the foot.

He found other interests at King's as well. The college library was the largest Hamilton had ever seen, and soon he was reading his way through it. Stories about great emperors and their wars thrilled him, but he was most fascinated by books about politics and economics. Besides the classic works on those subjects, Hamilton also devoured copies of debates in both the British Parliament and the colonial assemblies. He even founded a debating society to discuss the issues he had read about, squeezing its weekly meetings into a schedule so crammed with classes that he had no more time to write his poetry.

By the start of his second year at King's College, politics and debate had become a far more important part of Hamilton's life than medicine or mathematics. The North American colonies were becoming very angry about the way the British Parliament kept making up new taxes for them to pay. By law, Englishmen could only be taxed by a legislature of their elected representatives, yet the Parliament taxing the colonies had no American members. Up and down the east coast, patriots claimed it was time for the colonies to rule themselves. Their pamphlets, propaganda, and protests filled the streets and newspapers of all the colonial cities.

Hamilton, a British citizen by birth, had been brought up to be loyal to the king and Parliament. But the influence of his new American friends and the reading he had done converted him to the patriot cause. If Britain could break her own laws, argued Hamilton, then Americans had no reason to obey them either.

Hamilton published his opinions in New York newspapers in 1774. That summer he aired his views in person at a huge rally near New York's City Hall. Dressed in a long coat, a fine white shirt with lace cuffs, his reddish hair tied back with a slim black ribbon, the slender seventeen-year-old looked too young to be addressing the crowd of workingmen. Taken aback by the hundreds of faces staring up at him, Hamilton spoke slowly and hesitantly at first, but soon his beliefs conquered his stage fright. His call for freedom for the colonies appealed to the audience. As he finished speaking, a roar of approval greeted him. With a few words he had become a spokesman for American rights.

Despite his strong feelings, Hamilton could not tolerate mobs, and he was very loyal to his friends, no matter what their politics. One May night in 1775, a group of King's College students rioted on campus. Inspired by the skirmishes at Lexington and Concord which had begun the War for Independence two weeks earlier, they were out to tar and feather the pro-British college president. Holding their pine torches aloft, the students angrily tried to smash the college gates.

Hamilton was afraid of what they would do to his friend and advisor if they caught him. He forced his way through the crowd and climbed the stoop in front of the president's house. Sternly

he told his classmates that their behavior disgraced the very freedom they claimed to serve. A noble cause, he reminded them, deserved noble actions.

All the while the frightened president, in his nightshirt and cap, watched from behind his bedroom curtains. He was sure his star pupil was urging the mob on. The president was still clutching the curtains when Hamilton burst into the room, threw a cloak over him, and hustled him out the back door to the safety of a neighbor's house. The next night the president boarded a ship bound for England, thanks to a friend who had bound himself to America.

Hamilton calmed fellow students
who wanted to tar and feather King's
College's pro-British president.

Chapter

3

Student into
Soldier

Hamilton did more than make speeches and write pamphlets for the colonies' revolutionary cause. He had also joined a militia company. Every school day in 1774–75 he and his debating-society friends turned out to practice their marching and musketry in the local churchyard. Hamilton's unit called themselves "The Hearts of Oak." They wore short green jackets and leather caps which bore the patriotic words "Freedom or Death."

Hamilton enjoyed the practice immensely and rarely missed a session. But it is one thing to play soldier in a clean uniform when you know that once drill is over you will have a nice hot breakfast and a comfortable day in a classroom. It is quite another when the play becomes reality. By May 1775 the American War for Independence had begun in earnest. Real men with real guns were dying for what they believed. The Hearts of Oak would soon have to decide if they truly agreed with their motto.

The war Hamilton had wished for when he was twelve was there for him at eighteen, and he embraced it eagerly. As a boy he had wanted to fight only to improve his lot in life. As a young man, however, Hamilton had more than personal glory on his mind. He now wanted to free America from the tyranny of a British government that, by neither heeding nor respecting the colonies' complaints, had given up all right to govern them.

Hamilton's war began in New York in August 1775 when the Hearts of Oak captured the British cannon from a fort on Manhattan's southern tip and brought them to the American camp farther north. Despite the cover of silence and darkness, the British knew what was up. They were not about to let a group of young rebels steal their guns. From a warship anchored in the harbor they bombarded the Americans hauling the heavy guns up Broadway with musket fire and iron shot.

Frightened by the noise and smoke of what they feared was a British invasion, New Yorkers jumped out of their beds to hide in their cellars or to cram the streets leading out of the city. The panic and confusion of his fellow New Yorkers did not stop Hamilton. He calmly pulled his gun to American ground, and then returned to the fort to get another, as coolly as if the sights, sounds, and smells of war swirling around him were everyday matters.

Soon after this, Hamilton became captain of a regular artillery company in the Continental Army, headed by George Washington. Now he was in charge of recruiting, equipping, training, and leading soldiers to fight and die for America. Hamilton took his job very seriously. Although his men spent most of each day building a fort to defend New York City, their captain still made sure they had several hours of drill a week. Hamilton's troops, marching smartly in their blue and tan jackets, soon became known as a model company.

The men and their nineteen-year-old captain stayed in New York until August 1776. Then the hard soldiering began. Late that month the British demolished the American camp on Long Island.

By October they had pushed the Continental Army out of New York City and north into Westchester County. Four weeks later the Americans had retreated across the Hudson into New Jersey.

Nor could they stop there. The British kept after them, chasing them farther and farther south until on December 22 General Washington and a cold, hungry, tired force of twenty-five hundred men fled across the Delaware River to the temporary safety of Pennsylvania.

Hamilton's company stuck with Washington during that disastrous autumn. They were also with him when he decided to do something daring to renew American spirits and reverse American losses.

On Christmas night 1775, three days after ferrying the men into Pennsylvania, Washington ordered his army back across the Delaware to Trenton, New Jersey. There they were to surprise the British troops and the Hessian (German) regiments the British had hired to help them fight.

Hamilton moved his men out at eight o'clock that night. They marched through a driving snowstorm to McKonkey's ferry house where they waited for the little boats that would carry them over the ice-choked river. Once in New Jersey they still faced a 9-mile (14.5-km) march through fallen snow and falling sleet. Many soldiers had no shoes, and only tattered coats to protect their muskets.

The Americans struck the camp at dawn, surprising the Germans sleeping off their Christmas celebrations. With the first crack of the American guns, the Hessians ran to their posts, knocking over chairs as they pulled on their coats. But they were too late and too startled to defeat the Americans. Within minutes the Trenton garrison surrendered, and the weary Americans turned around and slogged back through the snow. Their stunning victory

Almost from the day they met,
Washington was like a father to Hamilton.

*Alexander Hamilton was a "born" soldier,
an officer and a gentleman.*

and their nine hundred prisoners made a wonderful Christmas present for the colonies.

Twelve days later Hamilton's company bombarded the British at Princeton and helped Washington push them back almost as far as New York. Then winter halted the war. Neither side could maneuver easily in snowdrifts and sleet. The Americans settled into their winter headquarters at Morristown, New Jersey, to restore their bodies and spirits.

Hamilton and his men welcomed the rest. They had seen a lot of action since September. Because cannons and other big guns had short range, artillery soldiers like them were always near the front lines. Not only did this make them easy targets for enemy fire, it also made them the first to be slaughtered when the enemy overran their position. The excitement and glory of battle came to these men only long after the shooting stopped. During active fighting all they knew was pain and terror.

Few American officers had been in combat as much as Hamilton. Despite the strains and stresses of his commission, however, he was always firmly in command of himself and his troops. The fellow officer who described him as a "mere stripling" who marched with his hat pulled down over his eyes, every so often stretching out to pat a cannon as if it were a favorite toy, did not know Hamilton very well. His boyishness was only skin deep. Inside he was a seasoned and trustworthy officer who took his responsibility to his men so seriously that even during the strenuous New Jersey campaign he kept detailed records of each soldier's pay and rations.

By his actions he was proving himself a man with no weak sides. It was no wonder, then, that while at Morristown that bitter winter of 1777, Washington promoted him to the rank of lieutenant colonel and asked him to join his staff.

Chapter

4

Washington's "Family"

General George Washington, commander in chief of the American forces, thought of his staff as his family. He called fellow generals his brothers and fondly referred to the younger officers as his boys.

These "boys" did indeed live like the children of the camp. They bunked together six or seven in a tiny room. Like schoolboys they spent their days at desks arranged around a large office, writing the endless orders, reports, and requisitions that keep an army going. They had no time off; Washington never relaxed, and so saw no reason for his aides to. Only at night could they enjoy some measure of fun and freedom. Then they were allowed to dine with the "grown-ups"—the generals, congressmen, or diplomats who were visiting the camp.

In this "family" of handpicked "relatives," Alexander Hamilton became Washington's favorite boy. Besides the great affection they had for each other, each filled a very special place in the other's life. Hamilton, whose father had deserted him, looked on Washington as the father he never had. For Washington, who had no children of his own, Hamilton was the son he might have had.

The two men were also bound by an astonishing mental sympathy. Their minds naturally ran along the same lines. Washington believed an aide should "possess the soul of a general." He wanted to be able to suggest an idea to that aide and have him develop it and carry it out. This Hamilton could do so well that he was called "the pen for the army," and all the headquarters staff came to treat any orders or advice from Hamilton with the same respect and obedience they would Washington's.

Hamilton spent four years at the center of the war with Washington. Not all of it was spent at a desk. In 1777, Washington sent him to borrow soldiers from other generals, and the money with which to pay them from other states. Negotiations took several months, but for all Hamilton's efforts the men arrived at Washington's camp too late to be of any use that year. Tired and discouraged, the commander and his newly expanded army retired to that year's winter headquarters, at Valley Forge, Pennsylvania.

Today we think of Valley Forge as the place where the American Army proved it had the courage and strength to survive the worst that any war has to offer. The men who camped there during the coldest, darkest months of 1778 were not interested in proving anything, however. They just wanted to stay alive, and that was hard enough. There was very little food, and even less clothing for the soldiers. The only shelters were crude and drafty huts of sticks and stones. Even firewood was in short supply. Many men froze or starved to death, and eight or ten others deserted every day. That figure would have been higher if more men had shoes. Even officers resigned their commissions and headed for home. Washington contemplated starting the spring campaign with a skeleton army.

Hamilton, shivering at his desk, blamed the misery at Valley Forge on the Continental Congress. He called the colonies' elected legislators "feeble, indecisive, and improvident," and accused them of being afraid to act. Why could not Congress, which had already acted for the nation by establishing an Army and a Navy, assume it had the power to levy taxes to finance the war? Hamilton also felt that a single responsible man, and not committees, should be in charge of all national affairs.

The Army's fortunes improved with the coming of spring and the arrival of two Europeans who would do much to alter the way the war was fought. The first of them was a German army officer named Baron von Steuben. With Hamilton as his aide and interpreter, Steuben took the weakened troops at Valley Forge and turned them into an efficient fighting machine. He taught them how to stand still, how to march quietly, how to use camouflage, and how to obey orders. The drills and regulations he used, and which Hamilton wrote down, are still the basis of army training today.

The other stranger Hamilton helped to help America was the Marquis de Lafayette. This young French nobleman had come to find fame and adventure helping the colonies fight for their liberty. He arrived in camp along with the news that France had agreed to send the colonies money, supplies, and troops to defeat the British. Lafayette and Hamilton soon were close friends.

Despite his new companions and his new duties, Hamilton was restless. He wanted to see action again. At the battle of Monmouth in June 1778, he had rallied frightened troops by rushing around the field on foot through cannon and gunfire, but this adventure had whetted, not slaked, his thirst.

Hamilton also wanted a promotion, or at least some special recognition for his work and ideas. He received none, perhaps because his ideas tended to be startlingly original. For example, in

1779 he proposed letting black slaves fight. Insisting that blacks could serve just as well as white, Hamilton also suggested that Congress "give them freedom with their muskets." Antiblack feeling was still too strong for Hamilton's plans, however, and so the nation that believed that all men were created equal denied themselves their brothers' help.

Afraid that his career was going nowhere, Hamilton dreaded another winter at Morristown. The 1779–80 winter turned out to be more pleasant than he had anticipated, mainly because many of the senior officers had brought their wives and daughters to camp with them. At least now the evenings could be given over to the art of flirting instead of to the art of war.

Charming and handsome, Hamilton captured many a heart that winter. But only one young lady captured his. He met Elizabeth Schuyler, one of General Philip Schuyler's five daughters, at a party, and soon a friend wrote of him: "Hamilton is a gone man." Just a few months younger than Hamilton, Elizabeth had a pretty face, masses of dark hair, a sweet disposition, and (wrote her admirer) "fine black eyes."

"I love you more and more every hour," wrote the love-struck soldier. But his ardor did not stop him from urging her to read more. Nor did his infatuation keep him from flirting with Elizabeth's pretty sisters!

On December 14, 1780, the two were married in the drawing room of the Schuyler house in Albany, New York. Holly and candles decorated the hall as the bride, her fashionable white wig draped with her grandmother's lace veil, approached the groom. Hamilton had exchanged his uniform that day for a black velvet coat worn over white silk breeches and stockings. His shoes sparkled with the rhinestone buckles that had been Lafayette's wedding

Mrs. Alexander Hamilton, née Elizabeth Schuyler

present. With the ceremony Hamilton gained not only a wife but also a family, an old and respected family that genuinely loved him. Another of his castles in the air had been built.

But even a happy marriage could not still Hamilton's need for action. Washington repeatedly denied his requests for a field commission, arguing that the young man was far too valuable in camp. Hamilton's frustration mounted until one chilly day in February 1781, when Washington chided him for keeping him waiting at a meeting. Hamilton instantly resigned from the staff, in his hurt and anger insisting that the two never were and never would be friends. The two soldiers sounded like schoolchildren squabbling on the playground.

Hamilton did not leave camp right away. Hoping for forgiveness, reconciliation, or even reassignment, he stayed on to train his replacement. When several weeks passed with no sign from Washington, Hamilton went home. There he prepared several papers about government and diplomacy for Congress and the press.

The rift between the two men lasted until the fall, when Hamilton finally got a commission to lead New York and Connecticut regiments to Virginia, where the British army was digging in for the winter. Rejoining Washington and Lafayette in Yorktown that October, Hamilton got his orders to take one of the British fortifications in the coming battle.

In the dark of the night of October 14, 1781, Lieutenant Colonel Alexander Hamilton raised his sword high above his head, slowly lowered it in front of him, and then led his troops into the last battle of the Revolution. He was the first of them through the trenches, over the parapet, and into the fort. Bayonets fixed, his soldiers clambered after him through the darkness and took the position in only ten minutes.

Other American companies attacked other positions at the same time. The enemy's defenses were completely destroyed. Their commander, Lord Cornwallis, had no choice but to surrender.

Hamilton's war service was almost over. His last duty was to arrange the formal surrender ceremony. At 1 p.m. on October 19, the assembled American army stood in formation as the British marched past, deposited their swords and flags in a heap, and departed to a tune appropriately called "The World Turned Upside Down."

Alexander Hamilton, his reputation as a hero now secure, watched the ceremony with growing impatience. With the last notes from the fifes and drums he broke rank, ran to his horse, and galloped home to Albany, where his pregnant wife waited for him. "Indeed," wrote his amused and fond father-in-law, "he tyred his horses . . . and was obliged to hire others to come in from Red Hook."

Chapter

5

New Life

Although the war did not end officially until the signing of the peace treaty in 1783, the fighting stopped at Yorktown. After the surrender, soldiers drifted away from the camps and battlegrounds, walking the highways and backroads in their ragged uniforms as they made their way home to family, friends, and the pursuit of their own happiness. The officers left the Army just as casually. They, too, were eager to get on with their interrupted lives.

Safely home with his wife in Albany, Hamilton considered his life. The war had not really interrupted anything for him. On the contrary, it had given him a national reputation as a writer, an administrator, and a brave soldier. It had also earned him the friendship of the ablest and most powerful men in America. The war had even brought him a wife! Now it was time to choose a career that would cap his good fortune.

By the time his first son, Philip, was born in January 1782, Hamilton had decided to become a lawyer. With his customary enthusiasm and energy he set about reading the books which were the basis of every legal education in those days before professional law schools. Hamilton allowed himself five months to do what took most men five years. Spending his days in the well-stocked Schuyler library with other students, at night he paced the parlor discussing the day's readings with lawyer friends. To help himself with the various legal forms used in New York State, Hamilton prepared a study guide to court proceedings. Published as a book, the guide was very popular, for it was the first time anyone had written down all the rules and regulations at one time.

Hamilton also shared his study time with the new nation by serving as New York's Receiver of Continental Revenue. In other words, Hamilton collected the taxes New York was supposed to contribute to the confederation of states. He was allowed to keep one-quarter of what he took in as salary, but unfortunately he could not collect one cent! New York saw no reason to send money to help South Carolina or Massachusetts or any other state, and Congress had no power to force it to. Hamilton was not terribly surprised by this. During the war, after all, he had seen the states' unwillingness to support even one soldier from beyond their borders. In fact, he had taken the job only because he thought it would help him lobby for tax reform.

He soon had an even better way of doing that. In November 1782 he gave up his post, packed his bags, and rode south to Philadelphia to take up his own seat in Congress. The young lawyer, who had yet to try his first case, felt bound to use his talents to "make our independence a blessing." Hamilton believed a congressman was not only a legislator, but also a "founder of an empire" whose job it was to establish a government, make useful alliances with other nations, and improve the nation's finances.

In Congress, Hamilton tried unsuccessfully to correct those defects in the confederation he had observed both as an army officer and as a tax collector. He served on many committees and led many debates, but had great trouble persuading his colleagues to do anything. Very few of them wanted to hear Hamilton's plans for a strong centralized government. The tradition of states' rights, which allowed each state to run itself by itself, was too strong in America.

Hamilton's arguments in favor of more taxes were no more popular. No one, then or now, wanted to pay taxes, but Hamilton proposed new duties on salt, tobacco, houses, liquor, even the number of servants one employed. He refused to back down from these. Without money, he warned, governments can have neither power nor security.

The present confederation certainly had neither. New York was not alone in refusing to pay its share of the nation's war debts. New York's governor even laughed at a Congress that could not enforce its own laws, calling it "King Cong." When four hundred Pennsylvania soldiers, angry because Congress still had not paid them, marched on the state house in Philadelphia, Hamilton saw how deep the country's problems really were. The government's ineffectiveness had almost cost the nation its independence, and now it was creating chaos across the land.

Hamilton was disgusted. He dreamed of a strong America ruled by a three-part government whose legislature, executive, and supreme court would guide and influence all the states. He even wrote his ideas down and circulated them among his fellow congressmen. But no one would listen, and so, after serving less than a year, Hamilton resigned his seat. He claimed it was because Philadelphia was too far from his wife and son. Actually he had decided that it would be more productive to stop worrying about public finances and work at earning money for his private life instead.

In the fall of 1784 Hamilton moved his family to a rented

house at 57 Wall Street, New York City, and opened a small office in the building next door. Wall Street, now famous for its bankers and brokers, was then full of lawyers, and many New Yorkers agreed that Hamilton was the best of the lot.

The Hamilton household continued to grow. Another child was on the way, and Baron Steuben, short of cash, boarded with his old army friend. Not that Hamilton had all that much money himself. Always willing to take on charity or welfare cases, and rarely refusing anyone's appeal for funds, he was nevertheless shy about demanding payment from his wealthy clients. Determined to support his family by himself, he took no money from friends or relatives, although he never sent back the shiploads of meat and produce his in-laws regularly sent down the Hudson River.

But as the law practice grew and prospered, Hamilton was able to treat himself to a few new suits with the brightly colored vests and lace trimmed cuffs he loved. He could also afford to go to the theater, or hear a concert, or buy a picture; on weekends he even did a little painting himself. He also built up his private library, adding volumes in French and German to a basic collection of classics and histories. But Hamilton was not always so serious about his recreation. He enjoyed tussling with his children and often borrowed popular romantic novels from the public library to read in the comfort and privacy of his own study.

When business was very good, there would be money for a servant or two, and then Mrs. Hamilton could have some time off. Her life was more like that of a farm wife than a society matron. She was the family's housekeeper, seamstress, and pastry chef. Besides taking care of the children (and in their twenty-five years together the Hamiltons had eight), she was also her husband's secretary. He tried out all his speeches on her to make sure they sounded right, and many nights she stayed up until dawn, revising or copying some report by sputtering candlelight.

During these years in New York, Hamilton became involved in two ventures very dear to his heart. In 1783 he organized a bank for his brother-in-law John Church and some of his friends. These men hoped to make big profits by supplying the money the bank lent. Hamilton hoped that most of those loans would go to the fledgling government to help it restore order and promote economic growth. Each man got his wish. Hamilton, with one share of stock, served as director until 1788; the Bank of New York still considers him its founder.

Hamilton's other venture was forming "The New York Society for Promoting the Manumission of Slaves and Protecting Such of Them as Have Been or May Be Liberated" in 1785. Raised in a slave society, married to a woman whose family owned slaves, Hamilton nevertheless gave his time and money to an organization that would free slaves and end slavery. Slavery had no place in his free and just America. Many of his friends, including Lafayette, now back in France, joined this movement to abolish what Hamilton called "a commerce . . . repugnant to humanity."

But for all his devotion to his family and career, Alexander Hamilton was devoted to his country more. After two years in private practice, he was elected to the New York State Assembly. The next year, 1786, he represented his state at the Annapolis Commercial Convention, where the states planned to discuss how to revise their individual trade regulations for everyone's benefit.

Hamilton was one of the few delegates who showed up. Evidently not even the prospect of making more money could make the states cooperate. Something had to be done before the Union dissolved into a bunch of squabbling states.

Hamilton, reading to his fellow directors the constitution
of the Bank of New York, which he helped found

Hamilton and his friend James Madison convinced the skeleton convention to call another meeting in Philadelphia in May 1787. There they would do more than rewrite shipping laws; they would reorganize the nation's government.

The cause Alexander Hamilton had been pleading since 1782 was being taken up at last.

Chapter

6

Selling
the Constitution

Once back in New York, Hamilton pushed the state assembly to select its delegates for the Philadelphia meeting as quickly as possible. By February the names had been chosen. Hamilton's was one, but to his dismay the other two belonged to men who did not share his opinions. Since each state would cast one vote, Hamilton feared his voice would never be heard.

In May 1787 the three men traveled down to Philadelphia and checked into the Indian Queen Tavern. On the 25th they, and fifty-two of the finest political thinkers in America, filed into the same room where the Declaration of Independence had been signed eleven years earlier.

After electing George Washington chairman of the convention, the delegates set up the rules and regulations for the meetings. The first was the secrecy rule, forbidding all reporters and visitors from the sessions. Members could keep notes on the speeches, but no one could publish them. This was to help each man try out his own ideas of government without worrying about pleasing an au-

*Hamilton played an active part in
the Constitutional Convention presided over
by George Washington in 1787.*

dience. Members were also told how to behave. They were not allowed to whisper, read, or pass notes while a colleague was speaking or they would be reprimanded by Washington himself.

These men understood that it would not be easy to create a government able to meet the needs and emergencies of a union of states. They knew that a truly effective national government needed the power to levy taxes, raise an army and a navy, regulate trade, and make laws that individual citizens would have to obey. And for a national government to work, the states could not be allowed to do certain things that might challenge its supreme power, things like issuing money, making treaties, waging war, or charging certain kinds of taxes. On these broad points most of the delegates agreed.

The men who came to the Constitutional Convention belonged in one of two camps. There were those who wanted to create a strong central government that left very little in the hands of the states; they called themselves Federalists. Those who believed in a weak central government that gave a lot of power to the states were Anti-Federalists. Hamilton was the lone Federalist of the New York delegation. How, he wondered, could these opposing views ever be reconciled into a union acceptable to all?

For four weeks Hamilton sat silently listening to the debates about the new Congress, occasionally taking notes on the back of a motion or speech. He was not happy with his friend James Madison's Virginia Plan which the Convention had tentatively approved. It was fine to suggest a central government and a two-house legislature, but Hamilton felt it was wrong to have the states, and not the citizens, elect the senators. Nor did he think Congress should choose the one-term-only president.

The plan offered by New Jersey was even worse. They proposed an updated confederation with a few more trade controls. Congress would consist of one house, and it would elect several presidents to serve at the same time. The delegates argued back and forth, unable to decide what to do with these proposals. Tired of the hemming and hawing, Hamilton finally decided to speak. Perhaps by explaining his ideas he could spur his colleagues to action.

June 18 was one of those unbearably hot and sticky days so well known to children awaiting the end of school. At 11 a.m., George Washington rapped the gavel on his desk to call the meeting to order, looked around the room, and nodded to his friend Hamilton. Clutching a few scraps of paper, Hamilton rose to speak.

His words sent the convention into shock. Hamilton's ideas were so outrageous, radical, and, to many, downright heretical that no one could believe his ears. The young lawyer from New York was actually suggesting that the central government be completely sovereign. The states, which he called inefficient and selfish, should have no power at all. Local interests should never compete with national ones, or states would be tempted to ignore federal laws and withdraw from the union. It would be far better, said Hamilton, to "annihilate the state distractions."

His fellow New York delegates were so angry they forgot to fan themselves. Hamilton continued. He wanted a popularly elected House of Representatives to serve three-year terms, and senators, chosen by special electors, to serve for life. This was too much like the British Parliament, with its elected House of Commons and hereditary House of Lords, to please men who had fought eight years to be rid of British rule.

Hamilton spoke on into the afternoon. No one moved as his incredible ideas kept spewing forth. Now Hamilton called for a court that could review or strike down any law that violated the Constitution. Then he spoke of the need to base any plan of government on the lowest estimate of human nature, and the worst that could be expected to happen. In an age that exalted the virtue of the common man, Hamilton was saying that people were basically selfish and silly.

His real bombshell exploded when he proposed that the president, also chosen by electors, should serve for life. He even referred to this leader as a monarch. A monarch! Did he mean the nation should have a king?

After five hours, Hamilton gave a little bow to Washington and sat down. No one said anything for several minutes. How could Hamilton talk like that and still swear that the establishment of a republican government was the one wish dearest to his heart? Finally someone cleared his throat and began to speak about another motion. Hamilton's speech was never discussed.

It did have its influence, however. His ideas were clearly the limit, and they made everything else, even the Virginia Plan, seem reasonable. The next day the convention voted to scrap the old Articles of Confederation and forge a new national government with three branches: legislative, executive, and judicial.

Satisfied that he had at least pushed the convention in the right direction, Hamilton left it to get on with its work and returned to New York for the summer. He was back in Philadelphia by early September with elaborate plans for the presidential electoral college we have today. He also worked with the Committee on Style to rewrite the various motions into a complete document. Much of the elegant phrasing and careful wording of the Constitution is due to Hamilton's literary skill.

The Constitution was the work of no single person. It was the product of a summer of compromise, of deals worked out over supper at the Indian Queen, or standing on the state hall steps. The final document pleased no one completely (especially Hamilton, who feared it was not strong enough), but all recognized it might work. In the end they all signed it, placing their marks next to where their state's name had been penned in Hamilton's careful script.

It was now up to the people to decide if this was the government for them. Each state held a ratifying convention. If nine states approved the Constitution within the year, it would become law. In many states approval was certain, but in others, especially in New York and Virginia, ratification could not be taken for granted. These big states, essential to the wealth and security of the new nation, were afraid of the central government's supreme authority and skeptical that it would help them at all.

Hamilton knew his own state's vote would be hardest to win, so he wrote a series of newspaper articles to explain the Constitution to New Yorkers and to convince them of its value. He asked two of his friends to help him with this task. John Jay agreed to write five essays about foreign relations, and James Madison contributed twenty-nine about the structure and powers of government, but most of the essays (fifty-one in all) were written by Hamilton himself. The first was published in New York City in late October 1787, and new pieces appeared several times a week thereafter through April. The three authors, writing collectively under the name "Publius," were so busy they rarely had time to review each other's work, and Mrs. Hamilton greeted many a dawn still preparing that day's column for the typesetter.

The essays, which were quickly collected into a book called *The Federalist,* center on three major themes that were very important to Hamilton: the need for strong leaders; the uses and limits of power; and the dangers of "faction and disunion." What had begun as a selling job turned into a commentary on the purposes and nature of the American government by three of its chief architects. As such, *The Federalist* is an invaluable guide to the Constitution which, although written two hundred years ago, still shapes our lives.

Hamilton's essays did a fine job of convincing the people of New York City to approve the Constitution but had little effect on upstate farmers. He would have to win them over with forceful speeches at the ratifying convention. This was no easy task. The delegates stubbornly refused to ratify it, even after New Hampshire had cast the vote that made it law. It was not until Virginia ratified that New York finally realized that by holding out it would lose the commercial advantages the other states would share. New Yorkers grudgingly accepted the Constitution in August, on the condition that another convention be called to draft the amendments we call the Bill of Rights.

Anticipating their joining the United States, New York City staged an enormous parade on July 23, 1788. Merchants, businessmen, furriers, shoemakers, tailors, and coopers assembled soon after dawn in the field where Hamilton had made his first speech twelve years before. Down Broadway they marched and pulled their floats. Even Nicholas Cruger, dressed as a farmer and leading six oxen, paraded in honor of the government his former clerk had helped engineer.

Although Hamilton was still at the ratifying convention, his family walked up from Wall Street to see the centerpiece of the parade, a fully rigged model ship, 27 feet (8m) long and 10 feet (3m) wide. As ten white horses pulled it down the street, each of its thirty-two guns fired a salute. Its figurehead and its name honored the man New York had to thank for this day—Alexander Hamilton.

Chapter

7

First Secretary
of the Treasury

Wearing a simple American-made suit, George Washington placed his right hand on the Bible and took the presidential oath of office on a chilly day in April 1789. The real work of governing the country had begun.

The Senate and the House of Representatives spent that spring setting up the government in the capital city of New York. During their first session they created the departments of State and the Treasury. Thomas Jefferson, the author of the Declaration of Independence, became secretary of state. In September 1789, Alexander Hamilton won Senate approval as secretary of the Treasury. His salary would be $3,500 a year.

Closing his law office, Hamilton took charge of the half-dozen civil servants assigned to the Treasury Department. Congress had asked them how to get the nation on its feet. Hamilton, sure that wise financial policies could strengthen both the economic and political health of the country, submitted the first of four reports that would answer that question in January 1790.

ALEXANDER HAMILTON
1757–1804
FIRST SECRETARY OF THE TREASURY

SOLDIER ORATOR STATESMAN
CHAMPION OF CONSTITUTIONAL UNION
REPRESENTATIVE GOVERNMENT AND
NATIONAL INTEGRITY

The Report on Public Credit ran to forty thousand words, and many congressmen complained that it was too hard to understand. The point of it was very simple, however. The United States had to establish credit so that it could borrow money if it had to. To do this, it had to pay off its old debts first. (Even today, before you can borrow money you have to prove to the lender that you can pay it back.) Hamilton proposed massive taxation to create a large fund of money to pay both national and state debts. His plan gave the government the money it needed to operate. It also bound the states to the federal Union by taking over their obligations.

The first Report caused a lot of argument, not so much about the taxes (which Hamilton called "debts of honor which the honest citizen must pay"), but about the assumption of states' debts. Most northern states favored it, for they had large Revolutionary War debts they were glad to be rid of. The southern states, with smaller debts, opposed paying for someone else's problems.

The Report stalled in the House of Representatives until a compromise on an unrelated matter was worked out. Over a fine dinner in Thomas Jefferson's candle-lit dining room, Hamilton and his former ally, now opponent, James Madison struck a bargain. If Madison convinced enough representatives to pass his program, Hamilton would collect enough votes to move the capital from New York, first to Philadelphia, and finally to the village of Georgetown, on the banks of the Potomac River.

A statue of the first secretary of the Treasury stands outside the Treasury Building in Washington, D.C.

In September, Hamilton, his wife, and their four children moved to a house at the corner of Walnut and Third Streets in Philadelphia. The second Report on Public Credit followed soon after. This one proposed increasing American revenues from foreign trade by taxing foreign imports. This tariff would also equalize prices so American products could compete with European ones. Hamilton had to drop this because farmers complained that a tariff would make their produce too expensive abroad, and thus hurt their sales. To take its place, Hamilton suggested a new tax on whiskey.

The Treasury secretary's third Report called for the establishment of a national bank. Because there were very few banks in the country at that time, Hamilton began by explaining what a bank was and how it operated. This bank was to be chartered and partially funded by Congress but would have little else to do with the government. Private stockholders would supply the rest of the capital. The bank would issue bank notes (paper money) that would give the nation a uniform currency. It would also lend money to the government and be a safe place for storing federal revenues.

The bank proposal, too, raised serious debate. The Anti-Federalists (Jefferson, Madison, and their supporters) charged that the Constitution made no provision for a bank. In fact, they added, Congress was not specifically allowed to charter any corporation. These men insisted that any power not precisely given to the federal government belonged to the states and warned against interpreting the Constitution too loosely.

Hamilton had not expected an attack from this quarter, but he dutifully went back to that document and prepared a lengthy defense. He argued that "there are *implied*, as well as *express* powers" granted to any government so that it may do whatever is "necessary and proper" to secure the general welfare. Chartering a bank, although not specifically mentioned, was constitutional because it helped promote the common good. President Washington agreed and signed the bill creating the bank. The public agreed, too. Within a few hours of its stock's going on the market, all the bank shares were sold.

Hamilton had one more Report to present. Having gathered and studied reports from China, France, England, and the New England states, Hamilton was pleased to see that Americans were doing more manufacturing than farming. He figured that more factories would help the nation grow by providing more jobs, more money, and less reliance on foreign goods. But his plans to encourage industry through government protection and subsidies were too far ahead of his time. An America that still thought of itself as a Garden of Eden rejected the idea that men could work anywhere but on the land.

American resistance also doomed the model industrial city of Paterson, New Jersey. There, at a site above the Passaic Falls, a corporation called the Society for Useful Manufactures was to build housing and factories. Workers would produce paper, sailcloth, stockings, blankets, carpets, shoes, and even beer. There were also plans to plant mulberry trees for silkworms.

But the project failed, and this Report turned out to be the only part of Hamilton's four-part plan that was completely abandoned. America was not ready to be the industrial giant it was destined to become. Most Americans agreed with Jefferson's opinion that farmers were God's chosen people, and that the nation would thrive only as long as its citizens worked the land. With his visions of cities and factories, Hamilton destroyed his countrymen's fantasies of rural peace and plenty.

His visions also fragmented American politics. Hamilton and his fellow Federalists believed in a strong central government, a loose interpretation of the Constitution, and an American economy based on trade, manufacturing, and farming. His policies reflected those goals. Jefferson's Anti-Federalists, on the other hand, championed states' rights, a strict reading of the Constitution, and a farming economy. Party clashes were inevitable.

So were personal ones. The dapper secretary of the Treasury, with his elegant clothes, refined manners, quick wit, and captivating charm sparred ever more frequently with the tall, freckled, redheaded, carelessly dressed secretary of state. Washington, fed up with the constant bickering at his cabinet meetings, took to seeing Hamilton and Jefferson separately. All three men, who together had given their time and talents to the establishment of the new nation, now began to long for retirement.

8

The Whiskey Rebellion

In February 1793 Jefferson tried to get Hamilton to retire first. Hinting that Hamilton had gotten rich from helping his friends buy bond notes and bank shares, Jefferson had an Anti-Federalist colleague open a congressional hearing into how Hamilton ran the Treasury, and demand to see all department ledgers, accounts, salary lists, and memoranda. Even though they had only a month before Congress adjourned to do it, Hamilton and his staff produced all the necessary papers and accounted for every penny. No one could prove him guilty of any misconduct.

The Anti-Federalists were keenly disappointed by the speed and thoroughness of Hamilton's defense. They had hoped to be able to "cut the throat of his political reputation in whispers." Jefferson immediately tried again, introducing a new set of charges and censures into Congress. This time he accused Hamilton of misusing government funds, of not reporting to Congress, even of negotiating a loan at too high a rate.

But Hamilton cleared himself once again. Only the diehard Anti-Federalists (or Republicans, as they now called themselves) voted for his ouster from office. The rest found no evidence of wrongdoing. Jefferson, miffed, complained that the Congress of "bank directors and stock jobbers" was sadly mistaken.

Hamilton understood these "malicious intrigues to stab me in the dark" were politically motivated. Jefferson's party had opposed all his economic plans, and by now the two were split over whether the United States should support the French Revolution or not. Hamilton realized that the stronger party, and not the stronger evidence, would win the fight for his office and his honor. Fortunately, the Federalists were still on top.

But the strain of his harrassment wore him out. Although in June he privately told Washington that he intended to resign, even that decision did not ease his stress. Weakened in body and spirit, in August he became a victim of Philadelphia's yearly yellow fever epidemic.

Hamilton and his wife were so ill that the doctors almost gave up hope. Their children, still untouched by the fever, were sent off to friends' homes and for several weeks could see their parents' pale faces only through an upstairs window. The Hamiltons were lucky to have a doctor who ignored the standard treatments of purges and bloodletting. Instead he prescribed bed rest, icy-cold baths, and lots of Madeira wine for his patients.

The Hamiltons were fortunate; they survived. Four thousand Philadelphians did not. As soon as they could, the Hamiltons went to recuperate at the Schuyler home in Albany. Along the way they stopped at an inn, changed into the fresh clothes the Schuylers had sent to meet them, and burned the old to make sure they left the fever behind.

The epidemic left Philadelphia in November, and by early December Hamilton was back at his post. Exhausted by his illness, he grew more depressed than ever over the investigation. He was proud that his fiscal program had restored and strengthened the nation's credit and economy. Congressional hostility and malice puzzled and hurt him deeply. Still brooding over it, in December he asked for a new hearing so that he could definitively clear his name. With the help of a restrained but blanket endorsement of all his action and decisions from President Washington, Hamilton got a unanimous clean bill of conduct from Congress.

Hamilton was so worn out from pleading his own case that he said nothing about Jefferson's departure from the cabinet just before the New Year. But even though he had begun to describe his own office as a prison, the prospect of serving without his enemy influenced Hamilton to withdraw his own resignation, at least for a while.

He spent the spring of 1794 advising Washington about foreign policy and preparing another massive report of Treasury transactions. Except for his eldest son, Philip, he was alone that summer; the rest of his family had gone to Albany to escape the yellow fever. They may have escaped the epidemic, but not illness. Mrs. Hamilton, pregnant again, felt weak and uncomfortable, and their two-year-old son, Johnny, suffered from a seemingly incurable fever. Writing to them sometimes three times a day, the worried former medical student prescribed cold baths, carriage rides in the open air, and brandy for the little boy. Johnny recovered.

Hamilton worried about more than health that summer. From the southern mountain states and western Pennsylvania came news of revolt. Farmers there were refusing to pay the whiskey tax and were even tarring and feathering the federal revenue agents who tried to collect it.

Hamilton's tax had hit them hard. Whiskey provided the only efficient way they had to transport and market their grain in the east. It was far easier for the farmers to distill their rye or barley and ship it, two kegs to a plodding packhorse, over the Alleghenies to where they could sell it for a dollar a gallon (3.8 l). Taxes of up to twenty-five cents a gallon were very hard for them to bear. Not only was there little cash in their frontier society, but the tax reduced their profits considerably. Alone out in the wilderness, these farmers felt they deserved more support from their government, not more hardship.

Hamilton thought the farmers were protesting more than just the tax. He thought they were resisting all national authority. Warning that giving in now would encourage others to disobey the law too, he urged Washington to quell the revolt with a show of military force.

Washington agreed with Hamilton's opinion that continued rioting could mean an end to American government. Although eager to preserve law and order, and willing to do so with all the powers the Constitution allowed, Washington preferred to try peaceable measures first. He promised to revise the tax law if the rebels dispersed. When during the following week, five thousand men demonstrated against the government near Pittsburgh, Washington knew this measure was not enough.

His next step was to call the state militias from Pennsylvania, New Jersey, Maryland, and Virginia to form a federal force near Carlisle, Pennsylvania. Since Secretary of War Henry Knox had gone to look after his property in Maine, the job of outfitting, feeding, housing, and arming nearly fifteen thousand men fell to Hamilton. He made sure that this force (which was larger than had been at any Revolutionary battle save Yorktown) was better equipped than the last army he had served in.

Pleading that he "ought to share the dangers into which his fellow citizens were brought" by his policies, Hamilton bought a

Farmers tarring and feathering a federal revenue agent
who tried to collect Hamilton's excise whiskey tax

new horse and set out with Washington to join the militia. He easily slipped back into his old role of "super aide."

As they had hoped, the Whiskey Rebellion was put down without any blood being spilled. The rebels fled to their homes, as Washington's troops marched west. "A large army has cooled the courage of these madmen," wrote Hamilton, "and the only question now seems to be how to guard against the return of the phrenzy."

His own answer to that was simple: leave a small force behind and round up the ringleaders. As Washington hurried back to Philadelphia for the opening of Congress, Hamilton stayed to oversee both arrests and tax payments. For this, people called him a stern punisher and military fanatic who denied the farmers their right of free speech. Once again he was puzzled by public reaction. Was he not just doing his job, which was, after all, to collect taxes? And had he not saved the nation from civil war or secession?

Returning to Philadelphia in late November under the protection of a bodyguard, Hamilton was met en route by a special messenger. The news was far more devastating than anything that had occurred in the past two years. Worn out by worry over her husband's safety, Mrs. Hamilton had miscarried their child and was now very ill.

Personal tragedy did what political plotting could not. On January 31, 1795, Alexander Hamilton resigned as secretary of the Treasury, and returned to New York to be a father, a husband, and lawyer once more.

Chapter

9

Out of Office,
but Not Out of Power

Hamilton was not altogether comfortable with his return to private life. He had grown accustomed to the power and pace of his work at the Treasury and now found the slower familiarity of New York too tame.

The cumulative effects of many bouts of fever did not help his state of mind either. The depression that often accompanies profound fatigue set his nerves and his temper on edge. Shortly after he left office, Hamilton's political gibes drove a Republican leader to challenge him to a duel. Only the quick thinking and quicker talking of their friends averted the bloodshed.

Fortunately his law office was flourishing. People had been clamoring for his services ever since the first rumors of his resignation had left Philadelphia, and he soon had an active and lucrative practice.

But nothing could keep him out of politics. Hamilton refused to seek the post of chief justice of the Supreme Court, a job that would have brought him great power and prestige, just to be able to keep his hand in party politics. To have to spend his life as an impartial judge would have killed him. A friend, amazed at Hamilton's preference for the New York Bar over the Supreme Court, finally shook his head and agreed that "politics will never be out of your head."

Nor could he stay away from the center of government. Among the wills, settlements, and depositions that covered his desk were always letters from the new cabinet members asking for advice about trade, commerce, credit, even what issues they should present to Congress. In effect, Hamilton helped to run the government from his law office.

This sometimes made him very unpopular. Before leaving office, Hamilton had advised Washington to sign a trade treaty with Great Britain in order to ease tensions between the two nations. Many Americans were unhappy with the treaty because they felt the United States had given up too much for too little. All over the country angry rioters burned copies of the treaty and hung dummies painted to look like its author, John Jay. When Hamilton tried to persuade his fellow New Yorkers that Jay's Treaty had bought the nation peace and time in which to grow strong, the crowd listening to him on Wall Street would have none of it. They booed and hissed their onetime hero off the podium.

Hamilton continued to work for the government in more personal ways as well. In 1796 Washington decided he had had enough of the presidency. He wanted to go back to being a gentleman farmer at Mount Vernon. After his first term, he had tried writing a speech to tell the nation how to proceed without him but could only come up with a rough outline. He had asked James Madison for help but was even unhappier with his version.

Now Washington took his unused "farewell address" and sent it on to Hamilton. As he had in wartime, Hamilton took his old commander's plain ideas and, after some consultation with John Jay, garbed them in elegant dress. The Farewell Address, published on September 19, 1796, cautioned his countrymen to encourage domestic economy, to avoid any permanent foreign alliances, and above all, to preserve and use their credit wisely. Thanks to Hamilton's care, Washington's words have guided American actions to this day.

The Farewell Address marked the beginning of the nation's third presidential campaign, and its first real contest. When the balloting was over on December 5, John Adams, the Federalist, had won the most votes and become America's second president. The Republican Thomas Jefferson came in second, and assumed the job of vice-president.

Even though Hamilton's friends still held important positions in the new administration, he was suddenly without a friend at the top. He and Jefferson were still at odds, and he had never gotten along with Adams or his wife, Abigail. The Adamses' hostility was personal, not political, however. It dated from the years when Washington preferred the advice of Secretary Hamilton to that of Vice-President Adams.

But Hamilton was not out in the cold for long. Within the year the United States was feuding with France over shipping rights and diplomatic insults, and it began to look as if America would have to fight. Hamilton urged Adams to negotiate for peace but, at the same time, to prepare for war.

Adams agreed. First he sent three diplomats to Paris. When their mission failed, he set about raising an army. He coaxed George Washington out of retirement to lead it by agreeing to the general's one condition: that Hamilton be his second-in-command.

Hamilton jumped at the chance to change his lawyer's suit

for an officer's uniform. Locking his office doors once again, he started recruiting twelve regiments to bolster the nation's small, weak, and poorly trained army.

It was as if the years had slipped away. Washington and Hamilton were in control again, and a very frustrated and hurt President Adams took himself off for an extended vacation at his family home in Braintree, Massachusetts. Fully aware that if war came he would lose all control of the government to those two, Adams urged his representatives to work extra hard at securing a peace treaty.

Hamilton was frustrated too. He was bogged down in the paperwork that went with trying to find shoes, guns, and blankets for fifty thousand new soldiers when he really wanted to be planning the defense of New York harbor. And even though Hamilton drew up a curriculum for an officer training school, and urged sending American troops to liberate Spanish colonies in South America, as the weeks went by he realized that his army would never see action.

But Hamilton soon suffered a far greater blow. One blustery December day in 1799, Washington rode out from Mount Vernon and got caught in a sudden hailstorm. He returned that night complaining of chills and a sore throat. By next morning his throat was so badly infected it had swollen shut. Within hours he was dead.

The nation mourned a great leader. Hamilton's grief was far more personal. He had lost a friend, an advisor, a second father. He now had no one to look after him, to help him, to protect him from his political enemies. The man who had made the foreign-born outsider a firm part of the American scene was gone, and Hamilton was now alone, vulnerable, and bereft.

For a while it seemed that Hamilton would take over as commander in chief, but a new treaty ended the need for the provisional army. In July 1800, Hamilton unlocked his law office once again.

He also returned to politics. It was another presidential year, and four men had thrown their hats into the ring: the Federalists John Adams and Charles Pinckney, and the Republicans Thomas Jefferson and Aaron Burr. Because of his hatred of Adams, Hamilton urged his fellow Federalists to support Pinckney. He even published several attacks on Adams, calling him vain, jealous, eccentric, and unimaginative. Hamilton's interference hurt his party badly. When all the votes were in, neither Federalist had won. Instead, the electoral college was evenly split between Jefferson and Burr. The election went to the House of Representatives, who could not break the tie either, even after thirty-five tries.

Here was a dilemma indeed. Which man was the lesser of two evils? Despite his opposition to all the man stood for, Hamilton knew Jefferson was honest and incorruptible. After fifteen years of dealing with Aaron Burr in courtrooms and army camps, Hamilton could not say the same of Burr. He used all his influence, then, to swing Federalist votes to Jefferson. Finally, on the thirty-sixth ballot, the tie was broken; Jefferson became president. Aaron Burr, who had come within one vote of that office, resigned himself to the vice-presidency.

Chapter

10

The Duel

In his inaugural address, Jefferson tried to soothe the political passions that had seemed about to destroy the United States. In his characteristic mumble, inaudible to anyone who sat beyond the second row, he announced: "We are all Republicans; we are all Federalists."

Despite the fine words, Hamilton knew that with Jefferson in the half-built White House in the new capital on the Potomac, his own political power was at an end. His party was split and out of office. This time the doors of his law office would have to stay open for good.

The new century found him busy in New York. He founded a newspaper, the New York *Evening Post*, both to report the news and to publish Federalist opinion. In a much altered form this paper still hits New York's newsstands every afternoon.

He also plunged into his law practice. Besides the civil cases and contracts that were the staples of his professional diet, Hamilton occasionally got to chew on a juicy criminal case. One of the most spectacular was his defense of a young carpenter accused of murdering his fiancée and dumping her body down a well. As the victim's body had been on display in the street, there was much public interest in this case. Every day curious citizens would cram the courtroom to hear Hamilton examine and cross-examine witnesses until his client was acquitted.

His most satisfying activity, however, was the planning and building of a house for his still-growing family. After years of renting dark, cramped houses in the crowded city, Hamilton bought 10 acres (4 ha) of land 9 miles (14.5 km) north of Wall Street on Harlem Heights. The plot had beautiful views of the Hudson and East rivers. He hired an architect to design the house. Two stories high, with the kitchen in the basement, the house featured big fireplaces, wide porches, and two octagonal rooms with long bay windows. In one of these hung George Washington's portrait.

Outside the Grange (named for the Hamilton family home in Scotland) was a pond, a river dock for fishing, woods for hunting, an ice house, a barn, and a chicken yard. In the garden Hamilton planted thirteen gum trees, one for each of the original thirteen states. He begged his friends for seeds of exotic fruits and vegetables, and in a constant stream of notes to his wife, he outlined his plans to plant bulbs, start a compost bed, and caulk the porch.

Building the Grange took most of his savings, but Hamilton was not concerned. His law office was bringing in enough to pay all his debts within a few years. In the meantime his family would be together and comfortable. Despite the three-hour commute to his office, Hamilton looked forward to spending many evenings with them in the drawing room, and to entertaining their friends at elegant picnics on the lawn. Further on he could imagine himself and his wife, gray-haired and doddering, playing with their grandchildren on the porch.

*The Grange, the home Hamilton built
in Harlem Heights*

Such happiness was not to be his. Even before the family moved in, Hamilton's dreams were irrevocably shattered. His eldest son, nineteen-year-old Philip, taunted a friend of Aaron Burr's at the theater one night in November 1801. The two traded insults in the lobby, and Philip challenged the other man to a duel.

Hamilton did nothing to stop it even though he loved his son dearly. He understood that the young man's code of honor could not leave a slur unanswered. The night before Philip ferried over to New Jersey (where dueling was legal), Hamilton advised him only to fire into the air and let his opponent decide whether or not to continue. His advice was for naught. Both drew and fired at the same time. By evening Philip was dead.

Gone was the boy a doting father had adored. Gone was the bright young college student, the kind older brother to a houseful of children, the mother's comfort. The entire family was devastated by the waste of Philip's life. Hamilton, who had lain down beside the boy to cradle and comfort him on his deathbed, was inconsolable. At the funeral he nearly fainted and had to be led from the church on the arms of his friends.

Nor did the loss stop with Philip. Their daughter Angelica, closest to Philip in age and temperament, went mad from the shock. From then until she died at the age of seventy-three, she remained perpetually as she was the day before the tragedy—a shy girl of seventeen, chattering to her brother Philip and sitting at her piano singing the Revolutionary War songs her father had taught her.

Hamilton never really recovered from the loss of his children. Depressed, he now believed that life was not something you tamed, but accepted. Religion became more important to him. Writing to a friend that "this American world was not meant for me," he planned to devote his time to scholarly pursuits.

His withdrawal from the world did not last very long, however. Within a few months he was back at work and back in politics. He had plans to bring new blood into the Federalist Party by wooing the working class away from the Republicans. And he hoped to get his party back in power through a new policy of compromise and concession.

He had another mission as well: to stop Aaron Burr. Burr's scheming and intriguing had already cut him off from the president he served. Shunned by Republicans, Burr courted the Federalists. In fact, while still serving as vice-president of the United States he ran as the Federalist candidate for governor of New York. Appalled by the man's "irregular and insatiable ambition," Hamilton got the Federalists to withdraw their support. Once again, Hamilton had blocked Burr's path to the top.

This was more than Burr could bear. On June 18, 1804, he wrote to Hamilton, asking him to explain some insulting remarks published in a newspaper. Hamilton refused either to answer or to accept responsibility for the offending words. Burr, unsatisfied, asked for a duel. Sick at heart, weary of life, and convinced that a duel, no matter what the outcome, would ruin Burr's career, Hamilton accepted. The date was set for July 11.

During the next weeks Hamilton made his will, entertained his friends, and saw his clients, all with no hint on his face that anything was wrong. At night he wrote poignant farewell letters to his family. "Adieu best of wives and best of women," he wrote to his wife. "Embrace all my darling children for me. Ever yours." Those few men who knew of the duel tried to dissuade him, but Hamilton was resigned to his fate. His calm was that of a man who had already given up on life.

Hamilton spent the night of July 10 in his Wall Street office. At 5 a.m. he rowed across the Hudson with a friend, a doctor,

Shot by Aaron Burr, Hamilton, following in his son's footsteps, died in a duel.

and his brother-in-law's pistols. At seven he and Burr met on Weehawken Heights in New Jersey. They stared at each other while their seconds loaded the guns, then stepped back ten paces and fired. Hamilton stood up on his toes, spun around, and collapsed on the ground. Burr looked at him for a few seconds, then ran for the boat that would take him to safety farther south.

Cradled in the doctor's arms, Hamilton calmly announced that his wound was mortal. A few minutes later he complained that he had no feeling in his legs. He lay motionless in the boat that carried him back to New York and was almost unconscious by the time he was put to bed in a friend's house. Despite the heavy doses of painkillers, he kept passing out from the pain.

Mrs. Hamilton and all the children arrived from the Grange just as crowds were beginning to collect outside the house. Hamilton saw his children come into the room, then closed his eyes, as if the pain of seeing them were greater than the pain in his stomach. His friends, his family, the people camped outside waiting for news were all filled with grief.

Hamilton lingered another day, and died at about 2 p.m. on July 12, 1804. He was buried on the 14th, a Saturday. Businesses were closed, citizens wore black armbands, flags flew at half-mast, muffled bells tolled throughout the city, and, out in the harbor, English and French ships fired their guns in mournful salute. A vast procession that included the mayor, the governor, congressmen, and Hamilton's horse, his master's boots reversed in the stirrups, accompanied the coffin to Trinity Church. There Hamilton was finally laid to rest in the America he loved so much.

And Aaron Burr? As Hamilton had predicted, he was ruined forever. Acquitted of murdering Hamilton, he later stood trial for treason for plotting to set up his own empire in Louisiana. He left public office forever in 1805.

Mrs. Hamilton survived her husband by fifty years, relying on friends for financial support, and died at the age of ninety-seven. She never allowed the memory of her husband to fade.

The next time you hold a ten-dollar bill, take a good look at the face that is printed on it. Probably no man did as much to make America the country it is today as he. Alexander Hamilton fought for the nation's independence, and then proposed a government that would keep it independent. His plans for building the economy of the new nation not only brought it prosperity, but also made it strong. Understanding that only with constant, careful nurturing could democracy grow and flourish, he worked untiringly for strong leadership and clear direction. And to save his country from plots that could destroy it, he sacrificed his life.

For Further Reading

Clarke, Clorinda. *The American Revolution, 1775–83: A British View*. New York: McGraw-Hill, 1967.

Cooke, Jacob E. *Alexander Hamilton: A Biography*. New York: Scribners, 1982.

Flexner, James T. *The Young Hamilton: A Biography*. Boston: Little, Brown, 1978.

Hacker, Louis. *Alexander Hamilton in the American Tradition*. Westport, CT: Greenwood Press, 1975.

Hecht, Marie B. *Old Destiny: The Life of Alexander Hamilton*. New York: Macmillan, 1982.

Hendrickson, Robert. *The Rise and Fall of Alexander Hamilton*. New York: Van Nostrand Reinhold, 1981.

McDonald, Forrest. *Alexander Hamilton: A Biography*. New York: W. W. Norton, 1982.

Mitchell, Broadus. *Alexander Hamilton: A Concise Biography*. New York: Oxford University Press, 1976.

Pancake, John S. *Jefferson and Hamilton*. Woodbury, NY: Barron, 1974.

Prescott, F. C. *Hamilton and Jefferson*. Darby, PA: Arden Library, 1980.

Welsh, Douglas. *The Revolutionary War*. Austin, TX: Galahand, 1982.

Williams, Selma R. *Fifty-five Fathers: The Story of the Constitutional Convention*. New York: Dodd, Mead, 1970.

Index